WORK FOR A LOSER !!!!

CRAZY QUOTES, JOKES AND ANECDOTES OF CORPORATE CHAOS AND CALAMITY

Claude B. Carter

Working For A Loser!!!! is published by:
alotta.edu, inc.
PO Box 392
Fort Washington, PA 19034

Copyright © 1998 alotta.edu, inc.

All rights reserved. No part of this publication may be reproduced in any form by photostat, microfilm, xerography, or any other means, or incorporated into any information retrieval system, electronic or mechanical, without the written permission of the copyright owner.

ISBN: 0-9662624-4-1

Material organization and copy editing by Adam Greenbaum and Claude B. Carter.

Illustrations by Paul O. Wilson.

Printed in the United States.

Dedication

This book is dedicated to Bosses.

You know who you are.

Special Thanks

I would like to extend special thanks to those people who made this effort possible.

Thanks to my father, mother and brother, and my wife and two children.

Thanks to the many friends who helped me...

charles, charles, cheryl, ted, brian, vernon, cleo, paul, herb, mike, doris, tom and gerry.

TABLE OF CONTENTS

PART I – CRAZY QUOTES & JOKES

Section One –
Bumbling Through With Low IQ   7

1. Managerial Wis-Dumb   9
2. Team Play–Led Astray   17
3. Blundering in Bits and Bytes   31

Section Two –
Bosses Behaving Badly   49

4. From the Mouths of Madmen   51
5. Sleazy Does It   61
6. Let's Belittle...Let's Be Cheap   69

Section Three –
Worker's Winning Moments   81

7. Closing With The Killer Comeback   83
8. Biting Zingers and Nasty Stingers   93
9. Spotting Defects in a Loser   109

TABLE OF CONTENTS

PART II – INSANE ANECDOTES

10.	Pinheads in Pinstripes	125
11.	Simply Insensitive or Insane?	139
12.	The Sweet Taste of Revenge	163

PART III – JOIN THE REBELLION!

13.	Nominate Your Boss to the "Loser's Hall of Shame"	175
14.	Liberate A Friend!	179

INTRODUCTION

Brace yourself for a big slice of life!

This book is about Bosses – amusing, dim-witted and cruel – as told by workers who deal with them. It is their contributions that fill the following pages.

This book is special because the contents are true. At times they are unbelievable, but stand as proof, once again, that life is stranger than fiction. It shows that Bosses create havoc, everywhere they go, on every inch of this earth. No matter how funny or sad you find your situation, there are legions like you, waiting to share an amazing tale.

In March of 1996, I was inspired to create the web site, *Working For A Loser!!!!* I thought it would be fun, and I wanted to give fellow workers like you, all over the globe, a voice and a chance to share your personal experience with all kinds of Bosses.

What started as fun, ignited a global reaction. From the beginning the web site drew critical and popular attention. It quickly amassed several prestigious on-line awards and a very loyal international audience. Surfers came weekly from more than 70 countries. They contributed thousands and thousands of real-life quotes, jokes, and anecdotes about every conceivable workplace and Boss.

So, after two years, millions of "hits" and endless requests, I finally succumbed to the persistent pressure to publish, in hard copy, the best of the best from the web site. I hope you like what we've done.

Because the contributors still work, somewhere out there, no names or e-mail addresses are linked to quotes or anecdotes. We did this, as we do at the web site, to protect the innocent workers who just want to vent their anger or share a silly tale.

The book is divided into three parts. The first part, CRAZY QUOTES & JOKES, is a series of chapters comprised mainly of hilarious one-liners and jabs at the Boss.

Part II, INSANE ANECDOTES, presents some of the funniest and most shocking real stories about Bosses and their actions. And Part III, JOIN THE REBELLION!, provides an opportunity for you to tell your tale and report on the outlandish behavior of some Boss in your work history.

Join the movement. Read the book. Visit the web site. Feel empowered. Strike out against injustice. From now on, when something isn't quite right at work, don't go postal, go to the web site – **www.myboss.com**.

Enjoy!

Claude B. Carter,
A Fellow Worker

PART I

Crazy Quotes & Jokes

– Section One –
Bumbling Through With Low IQ

Chapter 1

Managerial Wis-Dumb

Some Bosses are stupid – so stupid they're funny. Their bumbling attempts to improve a situation or solve a problem inevitably make it much, much worse. To these Bosses, we dedicate the first chapter.

Part I • Crazy Quotes & Jokes

TWEEDLE DUMB

After months of courting a high level manager at the Ford Motor Company, we finally got an appointment. To impress him, my Boss rented a Mercedes.

✳

My Boss was very disappointed when we didn't win the Federal Express account. He exclaimed, "I know the materials got there on time. I sent them by UPS!"

✳

My Boss voted against creating a Customer Service Department. He said it would encourage customers to complain more often.

✳

Chapter 1 • Managerial Wis-Dumb

✺

Convinced that he was about to get laid off, my Boss angrily told off his Boss. He got fired instead.

✺

After hiring a consultant to evaluate salaries, and spending more than $100,000 on the study, my Boss determined that only $7,265 remained for raises.

✺

One afternoon as a blizzard was raging, my Boss said, "Don't worry about the weather. We are in constant contact with the police. When the roads become too dangerous, we will close the office."

✺

Part I • Crazy Quotes & Jokes

✺

My company's sales are slow because our products are badly outdated. After a week long meeting of the upper brass, they decided to close the research and development center to save money.

✺

My Boss canceled the weekly status meetings on a long overdue project. She said, "Every week it's the same thing. Let's wait until something happens before we meet again."

✺

We hosted a dinner in our office for some very powerful visiting Japanese businessmen. My Boss was responsible for the meal. He ordered Chinese food.

✺

Chapter 1 • Managerial Wis-Dumb

✺

I work for a government agency and have a lot of contact with outside vendors. My request for business cards was declined. My Boss said, "Business cards are a personal expense."

✺

My Boss started a night time cleaning service called Domestic Partners. He gets a lot of prank calls and he can't figure out why.

✺

TWEEDLE DUMBER

After learning that his staff was fed up with unproductive meetings, my Boss called a 2-hour meeting to discuss the matter.

✹

We didn't know the company was in trouble until my Boss left the proposed lay-off list for a hundred employees in the company cafeteria.

✹

My Boss was angered by a recent performance evaluation that suggested he continue his education. He sent a copy of the evaluation to me with a post-it note attached. It read: "Is this dum, or what?"

✹

Chapter 1 • Managerial Wis-Dumb

✺

My Boss got a memo about skyrocketing copier costs. The memo pleaded, "Save money! Pass around company memos instead of copying!" Acting swiftly, my Boss called a meeting and handed out copies of the memo to each of his subordinates.

✺

My company has a permanent dress-down policy, except when we have a tele-conference with Europe. On that day our Boss makes us wear suits.

✺

Part I • Crazy Quotes & Jokes

❋

Rather than pay a $5 C.O.D. charge on shipments, my company developed a credit application process that costs the company $55 per order.

❋

With my Boss' new design improvements, we created "economy" car parts that were more expensive than our "premier" parts. To cover his mistake, my Boss labeled the new items "premier economy parts."

❋

Chapter 2

Team Play—Led Astray

This chapter shows how far bad Bosses deviate from being good leaders and motivators. These Bosses have a distinct talent for leaving employees confused about their objectives and unmotivated toward their work. Using their own words, let's see how bad "bad" can be, starting on the first day of a new job.

Energizing New Employees

"I hope you still want that job in my department. My first choice turned it down."

✸

"I see you've had no computer training. Although that qualifies you for upper management, you're under-qualified for this entry-level position."

✸

"You're our first and only black employee. Please, feel welcome and comfortable. We've all had diversity training and, frankly, I can't wait to use it."

✸

Chapter 2 • Team Play–Led Astray

Sharing Vintage Advice

"Once in my career I didn't get along with my Boss either. But when he told me how it was affecting my performance, I immediately did a 360 degree turnaround. I expect the same from you."

✸

"To have a successful career, you must understand that every job is 40% personality, 40% skill and 40% effort. Maintain that balance and you have the secret of my success."

Teaching Fair Play

"Never play favorites in your department. However, when you get a difficult project which may be unsuccessful, make sure you give it to someone who is vulnerable and unpopular."

"Budget control is your most important task. Throughout the year, never tell your employees about their shortcomings. Wait until their performance review. That way you can give out smaller raises."

Chapter 2 • Team Play–Led Astray

"Eeny, meeny, miney, mo,
Every paycheck we keep low,
If they holler, let them go,
Eeny, meeny, miney, mo."

Providing Crystal Clear Direction

"We have four, 15 inch computer monitors in storage. I want you to get the biggest one and put it in my office."

✸

"For the convention, get me three hotel rooms – one single and one double."

✸

"At the conclusion of this meeting I want your comments, both orally and verbally."

✸

Providing Praise

"We all work hard. So what?"

Spreading A Feeling of Equality

We have an executive washroom that requires a key, but there's only one toilet in there. Our executives would rather wait in a line outside this bathroom than go down the hall to the one with plenty of room, towels and toilets.

※

We organized our first company picnic to improve morale. At the picnic, grills were scattered everywhere serving hot dogs, hamburgers and baked beans. The managers had a secret grill with steak and lobster.

Part I • Crazy Quotes & Jokes

✺

At the end of a mediocre year, we were told that no pay raises would be awarded. At first we all took it in stride. Then we learned that managers eligible for bonuses could expect a 150% increase.

✺

My Boss was never very friendly until we were both promoted. Then he said, "Now that you're a manager too, we can be friends."

✺

Our CEO removed his e-mail address from the company directory. He said he got too many messages from "little people".

✺

Chapter 2 • Team Play–Led Astray

✺

Building Trust

My windshield wiper broke and I was late to work because I put in a replacement. When I got my evaluation six months later, my Boss had given me a poor rating. She felt my excuse was feeble. She said, "You lied. It didn't rain that day."

✺

During a staff meeting, we tried to define ways to improve our department's credibility within the company. My Boss said, "If we are skeptical concerning the viability of a project, we should express our concerns up-front, but proceed with the project. When it fails, we can say 'I told you so'."

✺

Creating Team Spirit

We were divided into four work teams, each with eight members. The teams entered a competition at work and first prize was eight baseball tickets. My team won. My Boss went to the next eight baseball games alone.

Showcasing Style and Grace

We were at a business dinner recently and started talking about family values and old TV programs. My Boss, a very breasty women in a low cut dress, turned to the Vice President for his favorite show. He looked up and said, "My favorite show was Leave it to Cleavage ... I, uh, I mean, I mean, Leave it to Beaver, that show with the Cleavers."

Chapter 2 • Team Play–Led Astray

✺

Rewarding Hard Work

I'm an event manager for a large corporation. After planning and organizing hundreds of events this year, my Boss gave me a poor review. He said I forgot to include forks in the fruit basket at the last event.

✺

For the first time in 10 years, I was late to work. A tractor-trailer had spilled chemicals on the highway during the morning rush hour. When I finally got to work–two hours late–my Boss confronted me and said he was going to dock my pay. I explained the accident. He said, "You should have listened to traffic radio before you picked your route to work. I did and I was here on time."

✺

My company conducted a salary review and then raised the pay scale for my level. I immediately met with my Boss because my current salary was below the new minimum for my level. To fix it, he reduced my level.

Recognizing Achievement

In February of this year I celebrated twenty years of federal service. About five months after the anniversary date I called the Human Resources Department and asked when I would receive the usual certificate and pin. They sent a blank certificate for me to fill in at my leisure.

Chapter 2 • Team Play–Led Astray

✺

Providing Leadership On Quality

I work for a software company that sells programs that crash frequently. I was telling the President about the repeated customer complaints when he said, "Be glad we don't make airplanes."

✺

Keeping Projects On Track

I am working on a multi-year project and my Boss asked for a project update. I told him I was ahead of schedule and about to finish early. He replied, "Wrong answer. Then what will you do?"

✺

Keeping Company Secrets

Our VP in the Human Resources Department was interviewed for the corporate newsletter. When asked whether there might be any layoffs in the future, she responded that, "... we must attract and retain only the very best professionals to distinguish ourselves in the marketplace. Obviously some layoffs will be necessary."

My company recently replaced the coffee machines with much smaller ones. Two days later we knew why.

Chapter 3

Blundering In Bits and Bytes

With the introduction of computers many Bosses fell behind, way behind. Is it lack of intelligence or lack of effort? Who knows, and who cares? The point is, computer incompetence can be very amusing and the blundering in this chapter is legendary.

Note: This chapter, at times, leans toward the technical. If you are not a computer geek and have no interest in computers, feel free to move on to the next chapter. We won't be offended.

Frantic Calls to the Help Line

"I think my new computer is missing a few items. I keep reading about a 'clipboard and scrapbook' and I can't find them in any of these boxes."

✳

"I finished writing this letter twenty minutes ago. I've been hitting the 'end key' since then, but nothing happens."

✳

"I put some extra memory in my computer but I still get the same math errors in my spreadsheets. What's the problem?"

✳

Chapter 3 • Blundering In Bits and Bytes

❋

"I just got another e-mail message from our office in Spain and it was still in Spanish. Is there a problem with our Internet connection?"

❋

"How do I save the whole document? This program just wants to save the changes. What good is that feature?"

❋

"If I get more memory in my computer, will I still have to save documents?"

❋

Part I • Crazy Quotes & Jokes

Chapter 3 • Blundering In Bits and Bytes

Stumped By Geek-Onics

When my Boss transferred to our department, we ordered him a computer with a Pentium chip. A little upset, he said, "I'm in no rush for a computer. I'd rather wait and get one without chips, dings or gashes."

✸

My Boss recently ordered a computer through the MIS department. His order read, "Please make sure my computer has the 'pinnacle' chip."

✸

While giving my Boss some computer instruction, she said we should not use the phrase "drag and drop" – it had too many aggressive and negative connotations.

We wrote an interactive program for a client that required a touch screen. My Boss rejected the concept because it was too provocative and she did not want to encourage "touching" in the workplace.

Request Denied!

After thorough analysis by our team of experts, the Boss decided not to buy the computers we suggested. She said, "I prefer the other ones – they're cute."

After buying one hundred copies of Lotus for the company, we were instructed to return every copy. My Boss explained, "It wasn't as easy as 1,2,3."

Chapter 3 • Blundering In Bits and Bytes

✺

After months of needs analysis and comparison shopping, our Boss overruled our computer suggestion because she thought the Apple logo was cute and symbolic of their recycling programs.

✺

Our new computers all came with black and white monitors. Since we had ordered color monitors, we were stumped. My Boss said, "I read the order and I changed it. Paper is white, ink is black, black and white monitors will do."

✺

My Boss attended an office automation meeting that would assign computers to people. He knew nothing about models, functions or machines. By the end of the meeting he objected to the machine he was assigned. He said, "I want a Power Mac. It makes the right statement about me."

※

E-mail Madness

My Boss thought his nasty e-mail message to the President was anonymous, until the President replied and requested an immediate meeting with my Boss and the personnel director.

※

My Boss called technical support because he couldn't send an e-mail message. The technician said the e-mail server was down and wouldn't be fixed for hours. In a very loud and rude voice my Boss said, "Next time idiot, send out a group message so we all know the problem."

Chapter 3 • Blundering In Bits and Bytes

✺

My Boss is having an affair with one of the office employees. I get e-mailed plenty of juicy messages meant for her lover. I'm "BobG", her lover is "BobD". I love the juicy stuff.

✺

To see if the company was reading our e-mail, I sent a message to a co-worker about a fake virus that might attack the computers and erase all the hard drives in the office. After lunch, that same day, there was an alert message on everyone's desk about the possible virus.

✺

Part I • Crazy Quotes & Jokes

✺

Trouble With The Media

As I passed my Boss' office, I saw him blowing on his computer mouse. He said, "I was working feverishly on this report and I think I over-heated the mouse. The arrow stopped moving on the screen and I'm just trying to cool it down."

✺

My Boss and I were traveling together for several days. One afternoon while we were together I checked my office voice mail for messages. He looked particularly fascinated and said, "You mean you can check voice mail while you're on the road?"

✺

Chapter 3 • Blundering In Bits and Bytes

✻

My Boss spent the entire weekend retyping a 25-page proposal that only needed corrections. She claims the disk I gave her was damaged and she couldn't edit it. The disk I gave her was write-protected.

✻

My Boss returned from his first spread sheet course beaming with self-confidence. He turned to me, the resident computer expert, and said, "You better watch out, now I'm an expert in EXCEL 1-2-3."

✻

After a successful day, my Boss said, "You know, I sent more than one-hundred faxes today and I never had to fill the paper tray, not even once."

Part I • Crazy Quotes & Jokes

※

Once, when his secretary was out sick, my Boss spent 15 minutes at the network printer trying to make copies.

※

When we were moving our data center to a new building, my Boss asked why we were backing up ALL the data on our mainframe. She said, "Why can't you just wait to see if anything goes wrong and then back up the bad ones?"

※

After four hours of scanning pictures, my Boss showed me her results. All of her pictures were poorly scanned and unusable. I asked her, "What do you think is the problem?" She said, "I think the scanner has a virus."

Chapter 3 • Blundering In Bits and Bytes

✳

My Boss is pregnant. She had her laser printer removed from her office because she thought it might harm her unborn child.

✳

My Boss was typing her resignation letter when her Apple crashed. The machine tried to re-boot, but after encountering errors it displayed an unhappy face. My Boss, seeing this, decided not to resign because she realized her machine was sad and would miss her terribly.

✳

I told my Boss that a virus had infected her PC. She said, "That makes sense to me. I was sick earlier this week, too."

Part I • Crazy Quotes & Jokes

✺

My department recently got its first scanner. When my Boss learned the news he said, "That's great! How many channels does it have?"

✺

My Boss recently bought some double-sided disks. When he got a "disk full" message he popped out the disk, flipped it over and tried to store data on the other side.

✺

My Boss recently ordered a computer with a fax modem. After it arrived, he called me into his office to find the paper slot for faxing.

✺

✹

My Boss said she was too busy for training on her new computer. To save time she took the tutorial CD with her so she could listen to it in the car.

✹

My Boss was furious. He said I gave him faulty instructions to find a web site. In a rage he called me into his office to examine the URL. It read :
www.webcrawlerNoSpaces.com.

✹

Is That A Hard Drive?

My Boss recently had a sexual harassment case at work. A member of our foreign staff was visiting our office. She was in my Boss' office killing time, waiting for a much bigger meeting to begin. After a few minutes she came storming out, shocked. Apparently my Boss had invited her to "play some games on his hard drive" and something got lost in the translation.

Chapter 3 • Blundering In Bits and Bytes

Byting Back!
A few byting chuckles.

My Boss is often MIS-directed. He...

❈

...doesn't do Windows.

❈

...bragged about a Pentium Macintosh he got for his home.

❈

...spent an hour in the bookstore looking for "XL for Dummies".

❈

...got an "out of memory" message and thought it was a temporary condition that would correct itself.

❈

Part I • Crazy Quotes & Jokes

My Boss is often MIS-directed. He...

✱

...won't get on the Internet – until there's one for managers only.

✱

...ordered optical drives thinking he would "see" the data on them.

✱

...won't use a computer until they're available in pastel colors.

✱

...needs a surge protector to buffer his mouth from surprise spikes in his brain.

✱

- Section Two -

Bosses Behaving Badly

"Piece of cake" is a figure of speech, you idiot!

Chapter 4

From The Mouths Of Madmen

This chapter explores the more shocking and vicious side of what Bosses say. We begin with a selection of nasty quotes from some of the meanest, most unsavory Bosses around the world.

That's Nasty

I told my Boss I dreamed about running the company one day. He said, "That's a manager's dream. Why did you have it?"

✺

Recently my father had a stroke. My Boss said, "That's an illness of a weak mind. I've noticed that about you, too."

✺

We complained to our Boss that our jobs lacked variety. He said, "Sheep don't need variety!"

✺

I asked my Boss why he talked down to me. He replied, "Be glad I talk to you at all!"

Chapter 4 • From The Mouths Of Madmen

✸

I asked my new Boss when I could take a break during my twelve-hour shift. He replied, "You got a break the day we hired you!"

✸

When asked to elaborate on the Company's benefit policy, my Boss sneered, "You work, you get paid – that is your benefit!"

✸

Signs There's Trouble Brewing On The First Day

"Over the years I've trained many people who eventually became my Boss. I guarantee that's not going to happen to you."

✸

Part I • Crazy Quotes & Jokes

"You weren't my first choice, but it's clear no one listens to me."

✹

"I see that your father and brother already work here. Considering their careers, wouldn't you want to try something more promising?"

✹

"Don't be alarmed, but I find your attire and mannerisms to be 'too ethnic' for our vision of diversity."

✹

I finally got an interview for the job I really wanted. After I was seated, the hiring manager said, "My son graduates from college in six months and I was hoping to save this position for him."

✳

After a short discussion which didn't include any comments about a savings plan, 401K, or other long-term benefits, I asked my new Boss to elaborate. He said, "Don't worry. You won't need long-term benefits for this job. I'll make sure you work again, long before that."

✳

Speaking of Diversity and Tolerance

When asked which session of a sexual harassment seminar he wanted to attend, my Boss said, "The one with no whining, fat chicks."

✳

Part I • Crazy Quotes & Jokes

✺

I told my Boss, a white male, I felt unspoken racial barriers were stifling my career. He said, "What you see as a glass ceiling, I see as a protective barrier."

✺

After we learned the manager of the Projection Department was infected with the HIV virus, my Boss quipped, "There may be openings in the Visual AIDS group soon."

✺

All new employees are assigned mentors, but after 2 months I still didn't have one. Since my immediate supervisor seemed like a nice guy, I decided to ask him. When I did he said, "Sorry, but it could hurt my chances for advancement if I was a mentor to a minority."

Chapter 4 • From The Mouths Of Madmen

✹

My Boss was complaining about the time I spent taking my wife to her leukemia treatments. He said, "Look, we're all going to die someday. Make sure your career doesn't die first."

✹

My Boss was searching the office, looking for an employee who frequently misses time after her radiation treatments. This time, however, she was at the funeral of a family member. When my Boss heard this he replied, "It's always something with her, isn't it?"

✹

My Boss recently interviewed a woman who hadn't worked in months. At the end of the interview he decided to give her some professional advice. He said, "You know, you are a little heavy. Don't you know Canadian employers look down on obesity, especially in women? That's probably why you can't find work."

Sharing Those Razor-Sharp Interpersonal Skills

You approach your Boss, hoping to gain some enlightenment or share a peaceful greeting. Surprisingly, you're greeted by...

"I don't care how your weekend was and I wish you would stop asking about mine!"

Chapter 4 • From The Mouths Of Madmen

✸

"In the future, don't share your suggestions. I pay you to do, not to think!"

✸

"I know there's low morale in my department. What's the point?"

✸

"I'm sorry if I ever gave you the impression I cared. I don't!"

✸

Chapter 5

Sleazy Does It

These Bosses lack character. They never make the right, fair or just decision. They will steal your good ideas and openly mock your bad ones. They are cowards looking for the easy way out.

We've all experienced these losers. Prepare to be shocked!

For Some, Sleazy Is Easy

I work for a family-owned check cashing company. When I was robbed at gun point, the owners deducted the stolen cash from my paycheck. They said I was in charge and I complied with the gunman's demands.

✺

Last Secretary's Day, my Boss gave me a dozen roses in a beautiful vase. Three days later she asked for the vase. She said, "The vase was not part of the gift. I want it back."

✺

It was raining heavily and my Boss sent me to his car to get some files. As I left his office, I asked to use his umbrella. He said, "No."

Chapter 5 • Sleazy Does It

✸

In a meeting not scheduled to discuss my performance, my Boss said, "I've been secretly listening to your phone calls lately and, quite frankly, a lot of them sound like personal calls to me. Can you explain that?"

✸

Recently I was driving my Boss around because he had a DUI conviction. While we were in the car he said, "People are really over-reacting to this DUI thing. They think I have a problem because I carry a flask with me. Hey, would you like a sip?"

✸

My Boss received a bomb threat. He reported it to the police but neglected to inform any of his employees.

Ethically Challenged

Rather than fix known problems with our products, the Executive Committee decided to reduce the warranty period.

✹

A co-worker died in a gruesome car accident at 11:00 AM. At 1:00 PM my Boss was taking things from the dead man's office to improve the appearance of his own.

✹

On the same day my company fired 372 employees, the CEO, CFO, and COO showed up with bright, new company cars.

✹

In response to very strong objections, my Boss said, "If you were really a team player,

Chapter 5 • Sleazy Does It

you would not see these 'adjustments' as unethical."

✹

At my exit interview my Boss said, "Your layoff has nothing to do with the favoritism you cited concerning me in the recent, confidential employee survey."

✹

While on a business trip, my Boss called to say I was the latest victim of downsizing. When he didn't reach me, he left my termination notice with the hotel operator!

✹

Shortly after my Boss became Director of the company's free food program, he said, "Let's think of a way to charge the homeless."

Any Way To The Top

After an important presentation in front of three VPs, I asked my Boss why he repeatedly asked me difficult and complicated questions which he knew the team hadn't answered yet. He said, "I wanted to show my Boss I was thinking."

❋

A Family Rule

Our company has a strict drug policy. All new employees must be tested. This rule was never broken until we hired this summer's interns and the President's son was one of them.

❋

During my interview, the head of personnel said, "We're only hiring one summer intern this year and we won't start interviewing candidates for that position until the Boss' daughter finishes her summer classes."

※

On The Firing Line

My Boss recently fired a gay employee. He called it "canning the fruit."

※

After firing several minorities, my Boss said, "I think that 'worked out the kinks' in our operation. I see only smooth sailing ahead."

※

Chapter 6

Let's Belittle...
Let's Be Cheap

A salary review is a particularly stressful time for employees. It is made much worse if you have a Boss like the ones represented in this chapter. They are cheap. They deny your achievements and value. But most of all, they seem to enjoy their power over you and your money. Make sure you are in a calm and peaceful state of mind when you read this chapter. It might just push you over the edge.

Subtle Hints It's Time To Quit

Performance reviews make us all nervous. But imagine sitting there, before your Boss, and hearing him say...

❋

"I know your performance review is due, but let's wait until tomorrow. I'm not in the mood for all that negativity today."

❋

"I made a list of the pros and cons of having you in my department and, quite frankly, the pro list is very, very short."

❋

"Under most circumstances, you'd be an outstanding employee. But I find you annoying."

❋

Chapter 6 • Let's Belittle...Let's Be Cheap

"You want my thoughts about your future? Well, it's not what it used to be."

✺

"It seems you're an over-achiever and that's upsetting to me and the other team members."

✺

Less Subtle Hints

Lately things have been less than ideal, but you had no idea they were as bad as this. His comments shock you back to reality when he says...

✺

"When you transferred into my department, I didn't have high expectations for you, and you clearly lived up to my predictions."

✻

"For the coming year, your professional objective should be to transfer to another department. I'd say as soon as possible."

✻

"How about a metaphor? To me, your career is like a 0% loan. I have no interest in it, and I no longer want it in my portfolio."

✻

"With all the experience you gained here, you'd make a great consultant."

✻

"You know, the best time to look for a new job is while you still have one."

✻

Chapter 6 • Let's Belittle...Let's Be Cheap

"You don't have a career. You have a job. Just try doing it!"

✺

Not Time To Be Sentimental

You know it's over, but you hope the termination interview will maintain an air of dignity. Why did you think that?

✺

"In my desk I have your fifteen-year anniversary pin. Human Resources sent it up today. I guess they didn't know I was going to lay you off."

✺

"I fired you because I saw your resume in the trash. You cocked the gun, I pulled the trigger."

"I see my hints throughout the year didn't register. Now it's come to this."

"Simply said, you're somewhat of a misfit."

"I have no parting comments. Bye."

The "No Raise" Set-Up

Getting no raise is nothing new. But sometimes you can hear it coming.

"Doing a great job just isn't enough anymore."

Chapter 6 • Let's Belittle...Let's Be Cheap

"Although we value your opinion, we don't pay for it."

✸

"You're at the top of your salary range."

✸

"You are a very valuable employee, but only outstanding employees got raises."

✸

"I did all I could but my hands were tied."

✸

"Management is looking at pay equity and they've frozen salaries for now."

✸

Part I • Crazy Quotes & Jokes

The Rationale

Knowing why sometimes makes it easier. That is, if it makes any sense at all.

✸

"By the time I got to people whose name began with 'P', quite frankly I was tired and I stopped awarding bonuses."

✸

"I've looked at this year's numbers and I didn't see anyway we both could get raises."

✸

"I never got a bonus in my first year on a new job."

✸

Chapter 6 • Let's Belittle...Let's Be Cheap

✺

"All nine of your co-workers, who had their evaluations earlier today, complained about their small raises and I made adjustments to make them happy. But now, all the salary budget is gone and I have nothing for you."

✺

"When I was a young executive, like you, I got a lot of raises I didn't earn. I see now that wasn't good for my professional development. But, as someone who is interested in your career, I'm going to see that doesn't happen to you."

Part I • Crazy Quotes & Jokes

"That extra $2.00 was a computer error!"

The Consolation

Riddled by guilt, your Boss tries to make you feel better about getting a puny raise. His attempts to console you are sadder still.

"Your wife works."

✺

"There's very little inflation."

✺

"You avoided a decrease."

✺

"It's still good money
for someone your age."

✺

"Next year should be better."

✺

- Section Three -
Worker's Winning Moments

Chapter 7

Closing With The Killer Comeback

In the past you have been tolerant and bit your tongue, but you can't resist this opportunity to pop the Boss between the eyes with a smart-ass remark, meant to bring him down a notch or two.

Go for it!

Occasionally the last word is yours. Thank the Boss for the leading question.

✹

"I've noticed that you never seek my opinion. Why is that?"

"If I don't know the answer, I know you don't either."

✹

"Could you be a character witness at my upcoming trial?"

"I'd love to, but the prosecutor asked me first."

✹

"Why didn't you invite me to your wedding?"

"It was a happy occasion."

Chapter 7 • Closing With The Killer Comeback

✺

"Do this for me, it's a no-brainer."

"If that's the case, isn't this job better suited for you?"

✺

"Why do you frequently correct me in meetings?"

"Because you're frequently wrong."

✺

"Where would you like to work next?"

"In a department with raises!"

✺

"The sign of a good manager is that he can stand at the front counter and do nothing."

"Well, you're doing a great job."

Part I • Crazy Quotes & Jokes

✺

"You think you are smarter than me, don't you?"

"The answer to that question is obvious – at least to me."

✺

"You submitted a stinging letter of resignation that doesn't make me look too good. Would you re-write it?"

"I've already softened it as much as possible."

✺

"I'll bet if you were keeping a file, you could charge me with several sex offenses."

"I'm not, but my lawyer is."

✺

Chapter 7 • Closing With The Killer Comeback

They Asked For It

I was asked to proofread my Boss' resume because she was looking for a job. I found many mistakes but I returned it to her unchanged. I said, "This looks fine. It represents you well."

※

I brought a thermos to an early morning staff meeting. When I poured some coffee, my Boss said, "That sounds like someone peeing into a cup!" He thought that was very funny and laughed for minutes. Then, one of the attendees asked how he could so readily identify that sound.

Part I • Crazy Quotes & Jokes

✺

My Boss received a memo about a weekend retreat with other company executives. After he read it, he said, "Why would I want to spend a weekend with these assholes?" "Maybe it's because you outshine the others?" I said.

✺

A group of employees at my office were clustered around the coffee bar eating cake. My Boss told everyone who walked up, "This cake is better than sex." After the third or fourth time this happened one of the more senior employees said, "Would that be sex with you?"

✺

My Boss called me into his office because he wanted to connect his Sony Discman CD player to his computer and run his CD software. I said, "Oh, only the Panasonic CD will do that."

✺

My Boss is the National Sales Manager for a network of office parks. For his birthday we bought him a hat with the words "Space Available" across the front. He loved it!

✺

Outwitting The Witless

We filled out a "completely confidential" survey about working conditions in our plant of 400 workers. Since I was the only black employee in the plant, I checked "white male" in the demographic section. One week later the personnel manager called and asked why I hadn't participated in the survey.

Part I • Crazy Quotes & Jokes

✺

After giving my Boss three frustrating hours of computer instruction with absolutely no sign of gratitude, I removed the printer cartridge from his printer and watched him walk back and forth for the rest of the day completely bewildered and unable to print his documents.

✺

I recently took a road trip with my Boss. When we got to the hotel, he said as part of his austerity program we should share the same room. I asked if his wife knew about this program. He then managed to budget a second room.

✺

Chapter 7 • Closing With The Killer Comeback

My Boss is very condescending towards computer professionals, even though she constantly needs our help. One day as I was updating her spreadsheet, I put an "X" in cell IV6000. Now every time she prints her work she gets a ream of blank paper until it gets to the "X". She's asked to have the printer serviced six times.

Chapter 8

Biting Zingers And Nasty Stingers

This chapter is a collection of the sharpest and funniest jabs at the Boss. Every flaw is exposed and exploited. Every type of Boss is skewered. It is an unrelenting attack on Boss-dom and we should pity the Boss who winds up in the line of fire of this insult barrage! Well, maybe not.

Part I • Crazy Quotes & Jokes

SLAM!

No facial hair was the rule as long as the Boss was clean shaven. When she stopped shaving, so did we.

✸

My Boss hates market research. He thinks the facts might undermine his position.

✸

My company firmly believes in recycling–it's because we have no new ideas.

✸

We re-organized at work and added another group to our MIS department. Now accounting is MIS-managed too!

✸

Chapter 8 • Biting Zingers And Nasty Stingers

✺

Every year, my Boss starts his annual presentation with a joke. This year it was his business plan.

✺

Management left my Boss in charge. They wanted to see the worst case scenario.

✺

We had a power failure and my Boss didn't notice. He's always in the dark.

✺

We have a "No Smoking" office. However "fuming" is allowed.

✺

BAM!

My Boss is the result of a brain experiment gone terribly wrong. Someone tried to implant management training, morals and business ethics in a brain only big enough for confusion.

※

In my organization, if you're not part of the problem, you're working without supervision.

※

I have been working in a managerial experiment. My Boss is the placebo.

※

In my company, any person can have an idea, but it takes a Boss to get credit.

Chapter 8 • Biting Zingers And Nasty Stingers

✺

I asked my Boss to attend a brainstorming session. He said he wasn't qualified.

✺

Our Boss called a planning meeting. We called it a "tragedy session".

✺

My Boss became a consultant so he could help other companies lose money.

✺

My Boss considered suicide to end his managerial woes. I agreed with his conclusion and supported his course of action.

✺

Part I • Crazy Quotes & Jokes

Oops! Sorry Ma'am

❋

My Boss is a hands-on manager. Now he's a defendant.

❋

While on trial for sexual harassment my Boss said, "Honest, it was a pat on the back."

❋

When he decided to remodel the office, he hired five new blondes.

❋

He then created a career path for secretaries. It's secretary, executive assistant, mistress, mail clerk.

Chapter 8 • Biting Zingers And Nasty Stingers

✹

This rotational program has gotten him five new paternity suits.

✹

Deeply tanned, he returned from a very long business trip. Deeply tanned, his favorite secretary returned from vacation.

✹

My last Boss used her "favors" to advance her career. When we were bought by a bigger company we knew she was "Under New Management."

✹

HIS TALENT

✸

My Boss is a gifted inventor. Early in his career, he invented "the fluke".

✸

Recently, he created a business shoe for fat women. They're called plumps.

✸

With this kind of talent, he is destined for fame, maybe a spot in the "anals of history".

✸

Chapter 8 • Biting Zingers And Nasty Stingers

HIS EDUCATION

✺

My Boss has a degree in micro-management and an MBA in mismanagement.

✺

His business specialties are "Hide the Truth" and "Fudge the Numbers".

✺

He recently got his Ph.D. in marketing. His focus was self-promotion.

✺

He then mastered several languages. He speaks Kiss up to management, Lie to customers, and Yell at employees.

✺

HIS WRITINGS

My Boss recently wrote a book. It's called *The Low Impact Manager*.

✹

Because it was so popular with his peers, he's starting a lecture series –

- How to Gain Money and Power Without Working.
- Masquerading as a Manager.
- Assigning Blame.
- Gaining Their Confidence to Steal Their Ideas.
- Taking the Credit, All of It.
- De-motivation and Seclusion – The way to keep superior talent in your department.

✹

His Boss jumped on the band wagon and decided to write his business memoirs. His book is called *My Defecations*.

Chapter 8 • Biting Zingers And Nasty Stingers

HIS LIMITATIONS

✺

My Boss is constantly disoriented. It's from repeatedly butting heads with progress.

✺

He's also handicapped. He is deaf to criticism and dumb to new ideas.

✺

When opportunity knocked, it left him dazed and confused.

✺

Finally, he had a stroke of genius. It killed him.

✺

His Definitions

✺

Calculated Risk: Little chance he can be blamed if things go wrong.

✺

Good Judgement: Supporting his position.

✺

Off strategy: Something he didn't think of first.

✺

Rapture: Getting a bonus he didn't earn.

✺

Chapter 8 • Biting Zingers And Nasty Stingers

His Nicknames

✺

"Old Yeller"

✺

"The General" – because he's quick to fire.

✺

"MTV" – because he makes a lot of noise and never makes sense.

✺

"Stupid" – because that's the most appropriate description.

✺

– METAPHORICALLY SPEAKING –
If he...

...was a car he'd be a lemon.

✺

...was an energy plant, he'd be a power failure.

✺

...was an animal, he'd be an alley cat– or some other kind of pussy.

✺

...was a clock, he'd be slow.

✺

...was a plant, he'd be a weed.

✺

...was a joke...wait a second. He is a joke.

Chapter 8 • Biting Zingers And Nasty Stingers

If my Boss was a superhero,
he'd be "Polyester Man".

CHAPTER 9

SPOTTING DEFECTS IN A LOSER

Bosses come in many forms. This chapter honors this diversity by providing a series of sharp and useful one-liners designed to help you spot a loser in the workplace. The lines come fast and furious, and are guaranteed to make you smile or cringe. Be careful, you might find signs your Boss is a loser.

Part I • Crazy Quotes & Jokes

You Know Your Boss is Cold Blooded When...

He likes being called, "The Terminator".

✹

He schedules vacation
to avoid Secretary's Day.

✹

He visits the hospital
to bring you work, not flowers.

✹

He attends your mother's funeral
to verify she's really dead.

✹

He starts an office pool against
your return from maternity leave.

Chapter 9 • Spotting Defects In A Loser

You Know Your Boss is Unqualified When...

He consults tarot cards
before big strategy meetings.

✸

He's late to the company's time
management meeting.

✸

He uses a calculator
to check his spreadsheet.

✸

He thinks talking louder
makes his point more clear.

✸

He claims his computer crashed
whenever his work is late.

You Know Your Boss is Delusional When...

He's convinced you find him sexy.

✱

He creates a computer virus
to honor the Unabomber.

✱

He thinks his job is secure.

✱

Chapter 9 • Spotting Defects In A Loser

You Know Your Boss is Sleazy When...

He calls 900 sex numbers
from your telephone line.

✳

He schedules fire drills
to rummage through your desk.

✳

Your "bad" idea gets him a promotion.

✳

Your "private" meeting
becomes the latest office gossip.

✳

You Know Your Boss is Sleazy When...

You both work weekends,
but only he earns comp days.

✸

He makes two-hundred grand, but still
"borrows" money from you.

✸

He openly flirts with your wife
at the company picnic.

✸

Being a "team player" means
you take the blame.

✸

He farts in meetings.

Chapter 9 • Spotting Defects In A Loser

You Know Your Boss is a Racist When...

He thinks raising the minimum wage is a plot by liberals to attract more illegal aliens.

✺

He talks about his trip to Israel whenever Jewish clients are around.

✺

He talks "jive" to blacks.

✺

He won't raise money for AIDS because he's not gay.

✺

He calls his one black employee Otis, even though that isn't his name.

You Know Your Boss is a Sex Maniac When...

He gives new meaning to the term, "working stiff".

✺

He attends sexual harassment training to improve his techniques.

✺

He requires secretaries to take AIDS and VD tests to get into his department.

✺

He nearly comes whenever you suck up to him.

✺

Chapter 9 • Spotting Defects In A Loser

Mmmm. Merry Christmas.

You Know Your Boss is a Sex Maniac When...

He's against maternity leave but supports medical benefits for baldness and impotence.

✱

He wants to turn "casual day" into "naked day".

✱

He refers to the secretarial pool as his harem.

✱

His browser bookmark file is all pornographic sites.

✱

Chapter 9 • Spotting Defects In A Loser

You Know Your Boss Lacks Interpersonal Skills When...

"Are you stupid?" is his idea
of positive feedback.

✻

His therapist commits suicide.

✻

He wears a suit on casual day.

✻

After ten years, he still
doesn't know your name.

✻

He points out a typo after a complicated,
two-hour presentation.

You Know Your Boss Is Computer Illiterate When He Thinks...

..."hardware" is complicated "software".

✸

...USENET is the electronic burial ground for old web pages.

✸

..."shareware" is a chic reference to hand-me-down clothes.

✸

...an extended keyboard is for someone with big hands.

✸

..."spam" only comes in a can.

Chapter 9 • Spotting Defects In A Loser

You Know Your Boss is Insecure When...

He just turned fifty, for the
third year in a row.

✹

He's short and all his employees
MUST be shorter.

✹

His bald head is hidden under
one strand of hair, wrapped around
his head seventeen times.

✹

He must have the fastest computer in the
department, even though he never uses it.

✹

His favorite phrase is, "Size isn't everything."

Part I • Crazy Quotes & Jokes

You Know Your Boss Has Driven You Crazy When...

You seek Dr. Kervorkian
as your private physician.

✺

You check the obituaries
hoping to see your Boss there.

✺

You will cut off a limb,
just for the sick time.

✺

Prison seems like a nice change of pace.

✺

PART II

★

Insane Anecdotes

Chapter 10

Pinheads In Pinstripes

There are few things funnier than watching an arrogant and stupid Boss make incredibly idiotic mistakes. Get ready to dine to your complete delight.

Keystone Rent-A-Cops

I work as a security guard for a large hotel. One day, a shoplifter was reported in the gift shop.

As I crossed the lobby, I saw the culprit running for the lobby door.

I called over the radio for back up. My Boss and another security guard were driving back from lunch when they heard the call. They saw a male running from the hotel and pulled the car up on to the curb, yelled for the man to stop, leaped from the car and wrestled the man to the ground. He was quickly subdued.

Both my Boss and the manager were horrified when I radioed again to say that I had apprehended the shoplifter.

Chapter 10 • Pinheads In Pinstripes

My Boss had caught a jogger. He now has free nights at our hotel for life.

※

Quitting Time

When I resigned, my Boss asked for more than the normal two week period. He wanted as much time as possible to find a replacement.

Since my new job didn't start for six weeks, I agreed.

After three weeks I told my Boss I could no longer work weekends because I was moving out of state. However, despite my restrictions, he scheduled me to work all seven days in my final week of work.

Part II • Insane Anecdotes

"I can't work Saturday and Sunday," I told my Boss. He replied, "You've had the last two weekends off! You have to work or I'll fire you."

"I already quit," I told him. "I'm working this week as a favor to you!" "You're FIRED!" he shrieked. "Get Out."

Before I could reach the door my Boss caught me. He said, "You can't leave yet! You're not fired until the end of your shift."

❋

Brain Slump

My Boss is in sales and he thought we were having a serious sales slump. When his phone didn't ring for three weeks, he began to panic. During a meeting in his office I noticed he had plugged his phone into the data jack for the network computers. Once he knew this, he asked me to cancel the emergency sales meeting we were planning.

Defective Management

We moved to a new office building and got brand new computers on the day we moved in. After they didn't work on the first day, my Boss sent them all back and demanded new ones. Three days later the new computers finally arrived and they worked perfectly. This time we had electricity at the workstations.

Chicken or Egg

I was applying for an advertising job at a local radio station. While being interviewed by the station's general manager, I decided to ask a few questions of my own.

"What sort of area promotions are you planning for the upcoming year?" was my first question.

Quite proudly the station manager replied, "Being a new station, our strategy is to create a listening base first and then advertise."

※

Request Denied

I wrote a proposal to get some new software. All such requests must be approved by the Boss. After the proposal was submitted, my Boss was unhappy with its structure. He decided to re-write it himself to show me how it was done.

After several days of re-writing, I finally saw his copy. At the bottom of his version was a rejection stamp. After all that work, he turned down his own proposal. He said we didn't need the software.

❇

The Glow of Pregnancy

My Boss and I were invited to a party thrown by a client. The client wasn't very friendly and our plan was to befriend his wife. Before the party, my Boss divulged his strategy; "His wife is pregnant, and when a woman is pregnant she loves to be showered with attention."

At the party, we found the client and his wife in front of the hors d'oeuvres, gorging themselves. Turning to the client's wife, my Boss exclaimed "Look at you, ripe and ready to pop!"

My Boss turned to me and winked. His plan was unfolding perfectly and he was beaming. The customer swallowed his food and said, "I'm sorry, this is my mother."

❋

Monkey In The Middle

We have five large chillers in our building, situated in a row and numbered sequentially. One day the Boss came down to look at something on chiller three and asked the operator, "Which one is number three?"

"Uh, the one in the middle," replied the operator.

"Yes, yes, but the middle from which end?"

※

It's In The Data

I recently started producing reports that my Boss had produced in the past. I noticed that one month in the middle of a twelve-month cycle seemed unusually high with negative indicators. It just didn't seem right so I investigated. It turns out that my Boss had loaded the data twice by mistake and produced erroneous reports for that month.

Eager to show my initiative, I fixed the data and made new charts and slides. My Boss was horrified. He said, "Put things back the way they were. I sold management on an elaborate plan to fix the field problems that showed up in the data. I can't change that now."

Say What?

I was demonstrating a computer program to my Boss that allowed people to send information to a Braille printer to make the information accessible to the blind. He looked at me and said, "That is truly Great! How can we make this triumph accessible to the deaf?"

How Complicated Is This?

My Boss called me to report a problem with his printer. I arrived in his office a few

Chapter 10 • Pinheads In Pinstripes

minutes later to find the printer was out of paper. He said, "I was trying to feed in single sheets because the tractor paper looks bad." During the next few minutes I showed him how to set his printer to accept single sheets. Then I left.

The next day, he called with the same problem and again I explained the procedure.

On the third day, he called again with the exact same problem. When I arrived at his office he gave me a serious look and said, "You really don't know what's wrong with my printer, do you?"

✹

Circling The Block

At my office, only managers have keys to the building. Recently, the computer system crashed and some of my files were lost. I told my Boss that I would need to work late for a few nights and would, therefore, need a key to the building to lock up when I went home.

The next day, my Boss gave me a key, but told me I couldn't let any of the other managers know about it. He said if I wanted to work late, I would have to leave the building at 5:00 with the rest of the staff, then drive around for a while until all the managers had gone home. Only then could I use the key to go back in and get my work done.

✸

Chapter 10 • Pinheads In Pinstripes

Really Sick

My supervisor is responsible for staffing a large call center. Last Saturday while working the graveyard shift, I received a call from my new co-worker. She said she was ill and couldn't relieve me at the scheduled time.

I was sympathetic to her situation so I advised her to call our supervisor to make him aware of the coverage problem. She said, "I already have. He's here, sick with me."

✷

Huh?

My Boss was meeting with his Vice President. The VP said, "I spend most of my time explaining things to you two and three times before you seem to understand the task at hand. I see this as a problem."

"What do you mean?" my Boss replied.

✺

Chapter 11

Simply Insensitive or Insane?

Insensitive or insane? The jury is still out on this one. Either way, it's shocking! Reading these true stories about cruel Bosses and their nasty deeds will send a shiver down your spine.

The Key To Success

I work in Customer Service where we track each person's call volume and number of unresolved customer complaints. My Boss always has the lowest unresolved count. To learn his secret I offered to buy him lunch.

Before he ordered his meal he said, "When I get a question I can't answer, I put the customer on hold. Eventually they will hang up. When they call back, they're sure to get another representative and it takes them out of my count."

Now that's customer service.

※

That's The Ticket

A good friend of mine and I work for the same company. One day a vendor came in for a meeting and told me and my friend that he had two tickets to a big, sold-out concert. Although he wanted to give us the tickets, protocol dictated that he give them to our Boss.

Although she didn't know it, we knew she had the tickets and would not be able to use them. Hoping that she would feel magnanimous, we mentioned our excitement about this upcoming concert.

She said, luckily, she had two tickets. They could be ours for $40 each.

✸

Welcome Back

I was working at a printing company and one of my responsibilities was to proof copy. I had been on vacation and when I got back the Boss pulled me into his office.

Immediately he started berating me. He asked, "How could you miss such obvious errors? These mistakes are a reflection of stupidity!"

Shortly after his tirade, we discovered the mistakes were made while I was on vacation. Without regret he turned and said, "Well, it looked like something you would do."

※

Stuck At Work

I worked one summer in a discount furniture store as a stock boy. One morning I was moving furniture to the freight elevator for the morning delivery truck.

Chapter 11 • Simply Insensitive Or Insane?

After a few trips, the elevator suddenly stopped and I was stuck between floors. The doors could open about four inches and all I could do was call for help.

My Boss heard me and came running.

When he called the elevator repair service, he learned I would be stuck for several more hours before a repairman could come.

Armed with this new information, my Boss returned to the elevator shaft. He put his head to the small opening in the freight elevator doors and shouted down the news. He then said, "Since you won't be working for the next several hours, I punched your timecard out."

I was docked for being trapped in an elevator.

A Crummy Boss

In my office, we have a strict policy against food in work areas. My Boss ignores this policy and often uses his computer as a tray table.

One day he called me into his office and told me that his computer had stopped working. Around the PC, there were crumbs everywhere. When I opened the computer I was startled by a live mouse that had built its nest inside.

Because of the safety hazard, I had to report the damage and the user. My Boss knew he could be fired for this.

The next day I returned to my Boss' office to get the serial numbers, but he had a new computer. During the night he switched computers with a clerk. He said, "I'm too important to this office to get fired and we have too many clerks anyway. Who'll know?"

※

A Trusting Environment

As a way of increasing our orders, my Boss decided we needed to build more trust between our customers and the sales people.

One way he thought to build trust would be to reveal confidential information to our customers about their competitors. For example, knowing the size of their competitors' orders might encourage our customers to spend more.

When I questioned him first on the business ethics of revealing confidential information he said, "Don't worry. In most instances we don't have the real information anyway. Just lie and make up a number that you think will increase sales. Trust is just a business tactic."

※

Speak Freely–Take Two

As the President of the division, my Boss was well known for his people skills. "You must win the trust of the hourly workforce, if you are to be successful," he loved to tell me.

Recently, the plant was faced with a union drive. In order to determine who was at fault the President arranged for meetings with the hourly crew. It was planned as a private meeting so they could air their

Chapter 11 • Simply Insensitive Or Insane?

grievances confidentially. No supervisory or managerial personnel were allowed.

During the meetings I decided to visit the HR manager. I walked into his office, surprising him. He quickly closed the door.

After I was seated, he indicated that I should be quiet and then he readjusted the intercom. He was listening to the confidential meeting. The President had bugged the room and the HR manager was furiously taking notes. The President wanted to get revenge on the workers who spoke out.

✺

No Extra Mileage

I was telling my Boss about a November trip I was planning. I said I wanted to purchase a frequent flyer ticket for my boyfriend, but since we didn't have the same last name it wouldn't get past the airline.

My Boss suggested we use my father's driver's license for my boyfriend. That way we would look married. I said, "That would not be a good idea – my father wouldn't go for that." With a wondrous look, my Boss said, "Why, is he a prick?"

✺

Opportunity Knocks

As a recruiter, I was trying to fill a key position at a client company. The hiring manager with whom I was working had a sudden heart attack and passed away.

Chapter 11 • Simply Insensitive Or Insane?

I approached our branch VP to apprise him of the events. He looked at me, smiled and exclaimed, "That's great news!"

Thinking I mis-heard him, I said, "Excuse me?"

"That's great news!" he repeated, adding, "Now we'll be able to place two candidates at that company!"

✺

A Reason To Celebrate

I am a very light-skinned African-American woman. I have worked at my company with my current Boss for the last 5 years. At work we celebrate every holiday. We recognize Christmas, Hanukkah, Saint Patrick's Day, President's Day – you name it.

As February approached I thought it would be nice to recognize Black History Month. I was pretty excited about my suggestion. After I had formulated my plans, I stopped by my Boss' office to get his thoughts. As I eased into one of his visitor's chairs I said, "You know, I think it would be nice to recognize Black History Month this year." My Boss looked up from his work and said, "Why? We don't hire black people! Who would celebrate?"

※

No Good News Goes Unpunished

Several years ago, our plant went through a painful downsizing. It took some time, but eventually operations settled out and we started to show a modest profit.

Chapter 11 • Simply Insensitive Or Insane?

A local newspaper did a story on our apparent recovery. In the story, the reporter told of our staffing levels before and after the layoffs. The story was positive and upbeat.

Our manager sent the story to our corporate office. It went up the ladder, getting good reviews until it reached the top. The "big guy" noticed the current staffing levels, and promptly sent a team out to review our manpower and layoff more people.

※

Taking On A Challenge

I was hired as a language instructor at a vocational training institute. At the time, the school was on probation because the graduates were not finding jobs.

Part II • Insane Anecdotes

Since I had prior experience in employment staffing, my Boss asked me to help. I rose to the challenge. I created a job search program. I taught students how to write resumes, how to interview, and how to keep jobs. I found companies who liked our graduates and would hire them. The job statistics went up dramatically and the school was removed from probation.

After all this, I did not get a raise. I was furious. I said to my Boss, "You wanted results and I got them. What more could you ask of me?" My Boss said, "Yes, the students got jobs, but did they get careers?"

✺

Know Who's On Your Side

My Boss re-organized me under someone I did not respect. This new manager quickly had me at the end of my rope. I went to my Human Resources representative for advice in dealing with him.

When review time came, my Boss gave me very low scores for "Team Player". When I pointed out that I was the one who went to Human Resources to get things resolved he said, "See, that's exactly what I mean. You don't even realize Human Resources is not part of the team!"

✸

Sexist Logic

I quit my job as a Software Engineer when I learned that my two male co-workers, with less experience and less education, were being paid 20% more than me.

After I explained the situation to my Boss he said, "Those guys are grossly overpaid and it's a problem. But you should be happy. You're getting the market rate."

※

Great Expectations

I take great pride in finishing my work ahead of schedule. Therefore, when I was given an average rating of "Meets Expectations" in the category of "Deadlines," on a performance evaluation, I questioned the rating. After all, this was one of my strongest categories.

After objecting, my Boss said I should work harder to complete tasks earlier. Again I explained that I have consistently completed tasks well in advance of published timelines and therefore I deserved

"Exceeds Expectations" as my rating.

My Boss explained, "But I expect you to complete your tasks early, hence the 'Meets Expectations' rating is correct."

✺

Excuses, Excuses

My Boss gave me a below average rating for my yearly performance review. She explained this low rating was primarily due to my poor productivity for the month of September. It was way down and totally unacceptable.

She would not listen when I tried to explain that I wasn't at work in September. I was on maternity leave.

The facts did not faze her a bit. She kept the lousy rating and warned me not to make excuses.

Little Consolation

I work for a large communications firm. After some downsizing in our department a group of us went to the VP and asked about our job security. He replied, "You are 100% secure."

Two days later, we got pink slips for a month-end layoff!

The following week the President came to speak to us. He said, "I know you have gotten conflicting information in the past, but yours will be the last layoff for now. That should make you feel better."

Chapter 11 • Simply Insensitive Or Insane?

Stress Management

My young Boss was new to the office where I had worked for nine years and it was his first management position. One day he became upset with me and began berating me in front of other employees in the office. He said that I was stupid and lazy and that everyone in the office hated me, especially him!

I was so blind-sided and embarrassed by his tirade, I burst into tears. "And THAT is your biggest problem" he told me, "you're just too sensitive."

❋

Any Questions

Several years ago, the President of our company ended one of the quarterly all-employee meetings by asking, as he always did, if there were any questions. When no questions were asked he said, "I keep holding these meetings, and no one participates. I would like someone to ask a question." One brave soul raised his hand and asked a question.

Agitation slowly covered the President's face. He said, "Well, if you had been listening to what I just said, you would know the answer to your question. Any more questions?"

✺

A Blazing Tale

I worked as a secretary for a large metropolitan hospital. My five-year old son was in day care at a church just three blocks away. One day a co-worker ran into the office and screamed, "The church is on

Chapter 11 • Simply Insensitive Or Insane?

fire! The church is on fire!" Immediately, I ran out of the hospital. As I approached the church I could see the smoke, the fire, four fire engines and people everywhere. I was in a panic. I lost my shoe, tore my dress and dropped my purse looking for my son.

Luckily, on this particular day the children had gone across the street to another building for arts and crafts and all the children were safe. After finding my child, and praising God, I returned to work completely frazzled and disheveled. When I finally got to my desk with my son in tow, my Boss was waiting. He said, "You left your station without permission. That's three days off, without pay."

✹

Night Shift

I work evenings. One night I received a phone call from my wife. She said her father had just died.

I immediately told my Boss and requested the next night off. He replied, "Absolutely NOT! They don't bury the dead at night!"

✸

Too Much Trouble

My best friend worked with me for eight years as a temporary employee. This meant she wasn't eligible for benefits or anything else. However, she was still expected to work evenings, weekends and holidays.

About a week ago she died. Her supervisor asked my Boss, the Director of

Human Resources, to direct deposit her last check. My Boss said, "We don't like to do that with deceased people." "Well, please send her last check to her father," her supervisor requested. "We don't like to do that either. Since she wasn't a 'real employee', she has no beneficiary form and we don't know who her father is. I think it would be best if we just didn't pay her for that last pay period," my Boss said.

My Boss decided to be consistent, to cheat her in death as he had in life.

✺

By The Book

At my company everything is done by the book. According to the rules, death benefits allow three days off from the day of death to the day of burial.

When my sister died, I called my Boss to say she would be cremated. He replied, "Oh, she's not going to be buried, she's going to be cremated. In that case, you don't need three days off. See you tomorrow."

✺

Chapter 12

The Sweet Taste Of Revenge

There is truly nothing sweeter than revenge. In this chapter, we are allowed to vicariously experience some of that sweetness through the eyes of a few brave souls who took action against their sleazy, incompetent or cruel Bosses–and lived to write about it. Bon appetite!

Mousing Around

For five hours I endured my Boss' abusive remarks while I gave her private computer lessons. Finally, something inside me snapped. When she went to the bathroom I cut her mouse cable and threw away the cord. I knew she wouldn't notice.

When she returned, I gave her work assignments to complete.

The next hour was the most enjoyable hour of my life. I watched her push that mouse around – forward, backward, sideways. She even lifted it in the air. Nothing worked. She cursed. She screamed. She looked at me for relief. I told her this practice session was a part of the training. It would make her more comfortable and confident at the computer.

Chapter 12 • The Sweet Taste Of Revenge

Using the keyboard was the only thing that saved her sanity. She was able to eke out small successes, but the impotent mouse kept her confused. I loved every minute of that hour – her confusion, her anger, her lack of control. At the end of the hour, I suggested a coffee break and during that time I replaced her mouse.

When she returned, I suggested a refresher on mouse skills – the most elementary computer skill.

✺

A Hot Issue

After attending a safety meeting, we adjourned outside where my Boss, the company Fire Safety Officer, set a small, contained fire to demonstrate the effectiveness of various types of fire extinguishers. While demonstrating the CO_2 extinguisher, my Boss singed the hair off the backs of his hands and arms.

Next, he grabbed a foam extinguisher and overshot the fire three times, until the foam supply was exhausted. The small, contained fire was quickly getting out of control.

As time passed and the fire remained unchecked, my Boss became panicked and unsure of himself. Finally he froze with indecision. Then, I stepped forward and quickly stomped out the fire with my boots.

It was a great day.

※

Chapter 12 • The Sweet Taste Of Revenge

In Any Language

I work for a management consulting firm. My Boss is white and so am I.

My Boss stopped in my office as he always does, but today he wanted to talk about ebonics, something he wants to abolish single-handedly. I don't know what had provoked him, but he was on a tear and once he gets started on something he can never stop.

Halfway through his lecture, my Boss realized he was late for a meeting with his Boss, the Vice President – an African American. Not quite finished venting, he told me to come along.

As we walked into the Vice President's office, he announced, "I'm sure you agree, this ebonics thing is the dumbest

Part II • Insane Anecdotes

development to ever originate in the black community. Although it's little consolation, at least ebonics is only language – no white people will be hurt by this. It took plenty of time to reverse those dumb 'set aside' and affirmative action programs. I bet I wouldn't be reporting to you now if it wasn't for those 'liberal' years."

The Vice President, a very quiet and thoughtful man, listened until my Boss was done. After silence had reigned for a short period, the Vice President leaned forward and said, "You know, I really don't support the concept of ebonics either, but there are certain things that are clear in any language. I hope you are listening closely. You be fired!"

✸

Chapter 12 • The Sweet Taste Of Revenge

"Adios"

I was born in Cuba. When I was 11 years old, my family moved to Wisconsin, where I learned English.

I now work at a brokerage firm in Miami, Florida. I was speaking Spanish with another secretary, also of Cuban descent, when my Boss flew out of his office and into the boardroom. At the top of his lungs and in the presence of over thirty employees and clients, he screamed, "Shut up with that Spanish! We're in the United States, and the language here is English. Speaking Spanish is not professional and it is not allowed at this firm."

Less than five minutes later, my Boss was at my desk. He had an elderly gentleman with him. The man was a walk-in client from Argentina. He had $100,000 to invest but he didn't speak much English.

Without hesitation my Boss asked me to translate during the investment session. I said, "I'm sorry, I cannot do that. You said Spanish is not allowed and I want to be professional."

※

More Than I Could Chew

I work in a department store, and chewing gum while on the sales floor is forbidden. On this particular day, I took a ten minute break after doing makeovers on six people in two hours. During my break, I ate a cookie.

Unfortunately, I still had part of the cookie in my mouth when I returned to my counter. The department manager saw the

Chapter 12 • The Sweet Taste Of Revenge

bulge in my cheek and assumed I was chewing gum. Standing in front of me, like a grade school teacher, she held out the palm of her hand and said, "Okay, spit it out!" Naturally, I complied. I hacked every bit of that half-chewed cookie into the open palm she held before me. As I spit, a sense of joy ripped through me as that nasty goo oozed through her fingers and dripped to the floor.

※

PART III

★

Join The Rebellion!

CHAPTER 13

NOMINATE YOUR BOSS TO THE "LOSER'S HALL OF SHAME"

Would you like to expose some funny or atrocious act? Would you like to have it read by millions on the Internet? If the answer is yes, use the information on the following pages to pick your favorite method of story submission.

Part III • Join The Rebellion!

SUBMISSION METHODS

Seize the moment. Exposing a Loser can be a great deal of fun. Think about it and write it up. Please keep your submissions short and concise.

✺

Using The Internet

Crazy Quotes & Insane Anecdotes can be submitted on the "Submissions Page" of the "Working For A Loser!!!!" web site. The home page address for the web site is www.myboss.com. The address for the submissions page is www.myboss.com./submissions.html.

Use the submissions boxes to send us your contributions.

Good Luck.

Using E-mail

You can use your e-mail software to submit Crazy Quotes & Insane Anecdotes directly to us without going to the web site. Address your e-mail to: stories@myboss.com.

Use the "Subject" in your e-mail header to identify your submission as either a "Crazy Quote" or "Insane Anecdote."

Good Luck.

Part III • Join The Rebellion!

Using Postal Delivery

If you prefer to use the postal system to submit your Crazy Quotes & Insane Anecdotes, please address them to:

> Working For A Loser!!!!
> Crazy Quotes & Insane Anecdotes
> PO Box 392
> Fort Washington, PA 19034

Good Luck.

Chapter 14

Liberate A Friend!

We hope reading this book gave you a moment of joy and a brief escape from working. As a new member of the Rebellion, it is your duty to share this experience and find new recruits. Surely you know someone.

New recruits are everywhere–at home, at work and at play. Give a new recruit a copy of this book as their introduction, a gift or a kind gesture. Please use the forms on the following pages to order more. You can also order copies from the web site at www.myboss.com/orders.html.

Be a friend and tell a friend. Take action and liberate someone today!

Stay in touch and keep the Movement alive. Visit the web site weekly for new and outrageous tales.

Part III • Join The Rebellion!

ORDER FORM

☎ Telephone orders call Toll Free:
1(888)MYBOSS2 (or 1-888-692-6772)
Have your VISA or MasterCard ready.

➤ On-line orders: www.myboss.com/orders.html

✍ Mail orders – send this form to:
alotta.edu, inc., PO Box 392
Fort Washington, PA 19034

❏ Please send me **Working For A Loser!!!!**
Please print.
Name: _____
Address: _____
City: _____ State: ____ Zip: _____
Telephone: (____) _____

_____ books @ $12.95	$_____
Sales Tax (see below)	$_____
Shipping & Handling (see below)	$_____
Total Order Cost	$_____

Sales Tax – Add 6% for books shipped to PA.
Shipping & Handling – Add $4.00 for the first book and $2.00 for each additional book.

Payment:

❏ Check – make payable to: alotta.edu, inc.

❏ Credit card: ❏ VISA, ❏ MasterCard

Card number: _____
Name on card: _____
Expiration date: _____ / _____

Call *toll free* and order now!

Part III • Join The Rebellion!

ORDER FORM

☎ Telephone orders call Toll Free:
1(888)MYBOSS2 (or 1-888-692-6772)
Have your VISA or MasterCard ready.

➤ On-line orders: www.myboss.com/orders.html

✍ Mail orders – send this form to:
alotta.edu, inc., PO Box 392
Fort Washington, PA 19034

❏ Please send me **Working For A Loser!!!!**
Please print.
Name: _____
Address: _____
City: _____ State: ____ Zip: _____
Telephone: (_____) _____

_____ books @ $12.95	$_____
Sales Tax (see below)	$_____
Shipping & Handling (see below)	$_____
Total Order Cost	$_____

Sales Tax – Add 6% for books shipped to PA.
Shipping & Handling – Add $4.00 for the first book and $2.00 for each additional book.

Payment:
❏ Check – make payable to: alotta.edu, inc.
❏ Credit card: ❏ VISA,   ❏ MasterCard
Card number: _____
Name on card: _____
Expiration date: _____ / _____

Call *toll free* and order now!

Part III • Join The Rebellion!

ORDER FORM

☎ Telephone orders call Toll Free:
1(888)MYBOSS2 (or 1-888-692-6772)
Have your VISA or MasterCard ready.

➤ On-line orders: www.myboss.com/orders.html

✍ Mail orders – send this form to:
alotta.edu, inc., PO Box 392
Fort Washington, PA 19034

❏ Please send me **Working For A Loser!!!!**

Please print.

Name: _____

Address: _____

City: _____ State: ____ Zip: _____

Telephone: (_____) _____

    _____ books @ $12.95 $_____

Sales Tax (see below) $_____

Shipping & Handling (see below) $_____

Total Order Cost $_____

Sales Tax – Add 6% for books shipped to PA.
Shipping & Handling – Add $4.00 for the first book
and $2.00 for each additional book.

Payment:

❏ Check – make payable to: alotta.edu, inc.

❏ Credit card: ❏ VISA,   ❏ MasterCard

Card number: _____

Name on card: _____

Expiration date: _____ / _____

Call *toll free* and order now!